SPIRITUAL
JOURNEY

SPIRITUAL JOURNEY

40 Days of Encouragement, Reflection,
& Self-Examination

GREG NEMBHARD

XULON PRESS

Xulon Press
2301 Lucien Way #415
Maitland, FL 32751
407.339.4217
www.xulonpress.com

Unless otherwise indicated, Scripture quotations taken from the
New King James Version (NKJV). Copyright © 1982 by Thomas
Nelson, Inc. Used by permission. All rights reserved.

Scripture quotations taken from the Complete Jewish Bible
(CJB). Copyright © 1998 by David H. Stern. All rights reserved.
No portion of this book may be reproduced, stored in a retrieval
system, or transmitted in any form or by any means without prior
written permission of the publisher.

Printed in the United States of America.

ISBN-13: 978-1-54568-144-2

TABLE OF CONTENTS

DAY 1 – BELOVED

Deuteronomy 33:12 (NKJV)

*"The beloved of the LORD shall dwell in safety
by Him, who shelters him all the day long, and
he shall dwell between His shoulders."*

What is your spiritual journey, and what value do you find in embarking on a forty-day period of prayer and fasting? Is it to you a Noah-like experience: forty days of expectation for the Lord to open to you a window of opportunity to step out to a whole new world? Is it to you a forty-day climb to the mountain top, where you experience God's presence and sustaining love? Is it a forty-day journey into an unfamiliar territory where you encounter and conquer the "spiritual giants" in your life? Is it a forty-day retreat into the wilderness, where you can have quiet intimacy with the Lord of life? Or, perhaps, is it forty days of fasting and praying to strengthen your faith, and the journey through life being more dependent on the Lord than ever before?

Then what?

Yeshua (Jesus) spent forty days in the wilderness preparing to begin His earthly ministry. Three years later, during the same period, He set His face toward Jerusalem, where scripture would be fulfilled at the execution stake.

The Christian Church calls this Lent—the forty days leading up to the death and resurrection of Yeshua. Christians enter Lent with an eye toward Easter Sunday, often making a commitment to give up something during that period. It is a time of fasting, moderation, and self-denial. At the end of the forty days of Lent, many hope to emerge strengthened in their faith and commitment to the Lord. Others simply go back to the norms of life until the next Lenten season. If you are a Christian reading this, be the former and not the latter.

In this same period, Jews around the world set their eyes on Passover, commemorating the deliverance from bondage in Egypt. As it is written,

> *This will be a day for you to remember and cel-*
> *ebrate as a festival to Adonai; from generation*
> *to generation you are to celebrate it by a per-*
> *petual regulation. "When you come to the land*
> *which Adonai will give you, as he has promised,*
> *you are to observe this ceremony.*
>
> Exodus 12:14, 25

Whether you are Jew or Christian, make this season one that strengthens your faith and brings you closer to the Lord. You are His beloved. He will bear the weight of your burdens between His shoulders. Leave your troubles at the His feet and take instead what He offers, for His yoke is easy and His Burden is light.

DAY 2 – STEPPING OUT

1 John 4:10 (NKJV)

"In this is love, not that we loved God, but that He loved us and sent His Son to be the propitiation [atonement/sacrifice] for our sins."

H ave you ever started out on a journey excited about what lies ahead, that is, until you begin to think about the journey itself? That initial excitement may have been because you were told what lies ahead or what you imagined the reward would be, but not the details of the journey itself. Think about how jubilant the people of Israel were when Pharaoh finally said they could leave Egypt. Or Mary's overwhelming joy at the news that she was found favorable to be a mother to God's own son. Even Elizabeth, when she was pregnant with John the Immerser (Baptist), exclaimed, *"How blessed are you among women! And how blessed is the child in your womb! But who am I, that the mother of my Lord should come to me?"* (Luke 1:42b-43).

It wasn't long before the people of Israel were wishing they were back in Egypt, where the conditions were less than perfect but familiar. Mary, for her part, began to realize the journey she had begun when Simeon prophesied over Yeshua when He was presented at the temple His eighth day in the world—*"A sword will pierce through your soul also."*

3

Today, you may be more focused on your spiritual journey than you have been at any time in the past. Or it may be that you feel you are not as focused as you should be and would like to change that. At a certain point in the journey, some may decide to quit before reaching the envisioned destination. If you are at that point, have you considered the importance of holding fast to a commitment? Entering into a spiritual journey is more than a choice; it is a commitment, a covenant between us and God to make our journey more about Him than about ourselves. We are responding to God's love, not initiating it. God sent His Son on a journey already knowing the end from the beginning and the encounters along the way. If you knew exactly what would happen along your journey, would you even begin it? Would you send your child on a journey if you knew of the exact dangers along the way? God also knew the after-effect of sending His Son into the world: that many would be saved on account of Messiah's death. His approach is always from an eternal perspective, just as He is eternal; anything else is temporary. Today, if you are feeling discouraged, consider the long-term benefits of staying the course. Remember that He who calls you will sustain you for the journey and reward you for eternity. For *"He will enable you to hold out until the end and thus be blameless on the Day of our Lord Yeshua the Messiah"* (1 Cor. 1:8, CJB).

DAY 3 – CONFRONTING SIN

Psalm 32:1-2, 8-9 (CJB)

"How blessed are those whose offense is for-given, those whose sin is covered. How blessed those to whom Adonai imputes no guilt, in whose spirit is no deceit!" "I will instruct you and teach you in this way that you are to go; I will give you counsel; my eyes will be watching you. Don't be like a horse or mule that has no understanding, that has to be curbed with bit and bridle, or else it won't come near you."

I encourage you today to read slowly through Psalm 32 at least three times. Take time to examine the message for you in this psalm. Each new day is an opportunity for us to examine our spiritual health and to acknowledge, own, and confess those sins that slowly eat away at us. Guilt is like a cancer that eats away at our souls and is often a companion to unforgiveness. Take time to visit those things hidden deep within, those unrepented sins that impute guilt.

In the third verse of this psalm, David said, *"When I kept silent, my bones wasted away because of my groaning all day long."* This silence is the unwillingness to acknowledge and confess transgressions. Do not allow the discomfort of confronting your sins to stop you from the blessing that accompanies repentance. The Lord says that He will instruct and give us counsel. He encourages us not to be stubborn, *"like a horse or mule that has to be curbed with a bit and bridle."*

Stubbornness can cause us to refuse to go in the way that God is leading us. Today, if you hear His voice, and if you discern the Holy Spirit's leading, do not be stubborn. It is an unpleasant thing when the Lord is forced to curb us with a *"bit and bridle."* Today is the perfect day to acknowledge your sins and shortcomings; it is the perfect time to unveil your guilt and confess your offenses to Adonai, that He may joyfully forgive you. *"Blessed are you in whose spirit there is no deceit."* Receive and hold fast to the Lord's instructions, and He will rejoice in you!

DAY 4 –
INTENTIONAL CREATION

Isaiah 44:24 (NKJV)

"Thus says the Lord, your Redeemer, and He who formed you from the womb: 'I am the Lord, who makes all things, who stretches out the heavens all alone, who spreads abroad the earth by Myself...'"

Think about it: God formed you from the womb. That means you were intentional—a forethought—not an afterthought; you are a special product of His design for His purposes. At this moment, you may be more focused on your shortcomings than you are this special design, maybe even asking yourself, "If God intentionally made me this way, then why am I so...?" You can fill those blanks with whatever shortcomings you think God should have fixed.

While you are thinking about that, let me also ask this question: If you were making something unique for a special purpose, would it be more meaningful to you if that special something *looked* perfect or, on the other hand, if it did what you made it to do?

God, in His infinite wisdom, loves us and has created each one of us for a special purpose. He loves us so much that He has given us the ability to choose our own paths, but as a loving

Father, His heart is for us to walk in the path He has set before us. God says, "I am your redeemer," and, "I formed you from the womb." In Isaiah 41:13, He says, "*I, the Lord your God, will hold you by the right hand, saying to you, 'fear not, I will help you.'*" God has formed us for a special purpose and promises to help us carry out that purpose. I can't think of a better deal than that. The One who stretches out the heavens all alone and spreads abroad the earth by Himself, He will help you fulfill your purpose. Keep that in mind as you face today's challenges. The God who can do all things is holding your hand and carrying you along, taking you through this thing called life. Today, if you have doubts, fears, anxieties, take comfort in the Great Comforter. Trust in Adonai your God!

DAY 5 – REST

Matthew 11:29 (NKJV)

"Take My yoke upon you and learn from Me, for I am gentle and lowly in heart, and you will find rest for your souls."

What comes to mind when you hear the word "rest"? What does it really mean to rest? Think about the different ways this very small word is applied and the different meanings ascribed to it. Conduct an internet search on the word "rest," and you will see results like: to *"cease work or movement in order to relax, refresh oneself, or recover strength,"* or, *"to be placed or supported so as to stay in a specified position"* (www.dictionary.com). The previous phrase also paints a picture of death, as in "rest in peace."

We also use the word "rest" to describe what is left over. Rest is a vital part of the human experience, and our Father is so keen to our need of rest that He included it in the Ten Commandments. Of course, He also left in place the freedom for us to choose not to rest.

How is your lifestyle of rest? I suppose the proper question is, do you have a lifestyle of rest? When we talk about lifestyle, our minds conjure images of shopping malls, programs, hobbies, work, and all the activities that involve a "go" posture. Yet,

God intended for us to have a lifestyle of rest. Even the land is prescribed rest every seven years.

The spiritual journey is one that naturally emphasizes the importance of rest.

God also intended for Himself to be part of our rest. It offers a time when we can withdraw from the busyness of each day and have communion with Him. It allows us to take the focus off our worries and fears and turn to the One who can take them all away.

Yeshua said that if we take His yoke upon us, we would find rest for our souls. Doesn't that just contradict the nature of a yoke? A yoke is an instrument of work, used to bind two animals together to plow a field or pull a cart. Can one really find rest under the burden of a yoke? This is the great mystery and wonder of our God. He turns conventional wisdom on its head and gives us a whole new perspective.

In this life, our souls are often burdened under the yoke of busyness and the continued struggle to keep up with society. Yet, Yeshua stands in the way and says, "Come, sit with Me for a moment." He invites you and me to enter His rest and to leave the world behind, even for just that moment. Today, try to focus on resting in His presence without the distractions of this life. Rest in Messiah, and your soul will rejoice.

DAY 6 – SAMPLES

Psalm 34:8 (NKJV)

"Oh, taste and see that the Lord is good; blessed is the man who trusts in Him."

Companies often offer free samples to attract attention to their products and the company. The fact that this practice continues is a strong indication that the strategy has borne positive results. If you shop at certain wholesale stores, you know that you can almost count on the chance to sample a food item while you are there. The same is true for some restaurants in the cafeteria area of a shopping mall. There is a level of confidence in offering free samples, confidence that those who try will enjoy that morsel so much they will buy the product and return another day for more. Otherwise, it is a waste of resources.

So, what does this have to do with Scripture and our spiritual journey? Thanks for asking!

The Psalmist says try the Lord, but he goes even further, promising that we will see that He is good. The Psalmist is confident that our experience of even a brief encounter with the Lord will leave us wanting more of Him. Even if we fall away for a season, we often find ourselves desiring more of Him.

"Taste and see that the Lord is good," not "taste and tell me what you think."

There is only one conclusion one can come to when we encounter the living God, and that is He is good and righteous. There are those who refuse to even open themselves up to a conversation about God, for fear that they will agree. Others are simply dismissive of Him, deceived by the world and the flesh that offers momentary gratification.

Take this time to consider what the Lord is offering. If you do not have a relationship with Adonai, He is inviting you into one, but first, He says, "Just try me!" Today, if you know the Lord and your relationship with Him has soured or otherwise derailed, take this moment to consider the cause of that souring. It's as if He is saying to you, "I gaze constantly out the window, seeking to see you far off, that I might run to you and tell you that My heart longs for you." If you know Adonai and have ongoing intimacy with your Creator today, He is saying, "Come a little further, that I may show you wonderful things you have not known."

DAY 7 – YOUR WORTH

Psalm 34:22 (NKJV)

"The LORD redeems the soul of His servants, and none of those who trust in Him shall be condemned."

What comes to mind when you read this verse, and what other scripture resonates while you ponder this psalm? I recommend that you read the entire chapter and meditate on each verse; there is such a richness to each of them that we can only receive through prayer, study, and quiet meditation.

What immediately comes to my mind is what Yeshua said in Matthew 16:26: *"What do you benefit if you gain the whole world but lose your own soul? Is anything worth more than the soul?"* Psalm 34 promises deliverance for the righteous. We often only seek deliverance in the moment or season and often from things affecting the flesh. God, on the other hand, desires to save our souls. He is focused on life after death, while we are focused on life before death.

Psalm 34 also reminds me of what Yeshua said in Matthew 10:28: *"Do not be afraid of those who want to kill your body; they cannot touch your soul. Fear only God, who can destroy both soul and body in hell."*

The Lord redeems the soul. What is the condition of your soul as you read this? Are you confident that you will escape the fires of hell, or are you in any way doubtful? The wonderful thing about this life is that while we have it, we also have an opportunity to receive grace. The Lord wants to save your soul. Let me say that again; **The Lord wants to save you soul**! He who has the power to destroy wants instead to build. God wants each of us to have life after death, even if we ourselves aren't too concerned about it. God wants us to have a good life now and the best life afterwards.

Satan cannot destroy your soul but tend to lead you into surrendering it to him, thereby forfeiting life eternal. God will not act against our will. Even though He wants to save each of us, it is up to us to want to be saved. He will not act against our will.

Do you want life today and life later? It is up to you to seek it out. Yeshua said, *"Ask and it will be given, seek and you will find, knock and the door will be opened to you"* (Matt. 7:7-8). Think of everything you ask for each day, all that you seek, and all the doors you try to open or walk through. How much of that leads to the Lord? How much of it leads to life?

Today, if you have doubts, turn your face to the Lord and allow Him to wipe them away. Seek His face, ask His forgiveness, and knock on the doors of His mercy so that He may open the doors of heaven to you. Today, if you have confidence in your salvation, keep on asking, keep on seeking, keep on knocking—which is the proper rendering of that verse—so that the eyes and ears of Adonai may remain focused on you. Bless the Lord, and He will pour out His blessings upon you.

DAY 8 – A WORLD WITHOUT GOD

Mark 4:35-41 (NKJV)

"On the same day, when evening had come, He said to them, 'Let us cross over to the other side.' Now when they had left the multitude, they took Him along in the boat as He was. And other little boats were also with Him. And a great windstorm arose, and the waves beat into the boat, so that it was already filling. But He was in the stern, asleep on a pillow. And they awoke Him and said to Him, 'Teacher, do You not care that we are perishing?' Then He arose and rebuked the wind, and said to the sea, 'Peace, be still!' And the wind ceased and there was a great calm. But He said to them, 'Why are you so fearful? How is it that you have no faith?' And they feared exceedingly, and said to one another, 'Who can this be, that even the wind and the sea obey Him!'"

Have you ever wondered what the world would be like if there were no God? Seriously, think about it! As messy as this world is, if God didn't exist, or if He didn't care, what kind of world do you think we would have? We could look to Sodom and Gomorrah as an example of a world without God; it became a vile and wicked place to live.

I think the account of Yeshua asleep on the boat is an example of the chaos we would have in a world where God isn't active. This storm must have been really bad to make a group of fishermen fear they were going to die. Yet, the One who controls the winds and the waves was sleeping just an arm's length away. It wasn't until they roused Him that He spoke to the situation that was coming against them.

What storm is currently raging against you, and what is it that you are crying out for? The Lord knows and is very near to you; just call out to Him. Don't be afraid to rouse Him. While He is not literally sleeping, we must petition Him with vigor, fear, and trembling. *"Let us therefore come boldly to the throne of grace, that we may obtain mercy and find grace to help in time of need"* (Heb. 4:16).

Another example of a world without God is Yeshua's death on the cross. We see here what happens when the One who holds all things together departs from creation. In that moment when Yeshua died, the Father turned His face away. As Yeshua looked to His Heavenly Father, neither the Father nor the Son were looking on the earth, and it erupted; darkness covered it, and the ground quaked as the Light of the world gave up His Spirit.

Today, I encourage you to rejoice and give thanks that the Lord lives, that His Spirit is alive and active in us who have received Him. He does not sleep, neither does He slumber, and He is much closer than an arm's length away. Be open and honest about your circumstances and ask Him to speak to them. *"Rejoice in the Lord, delight yourself in Him, and He will give you the desires of your heart"* (Psalm 37:4).

DAY 9 – LOOKING AHEAD

Psalm 35:18 (NKJV)

"I will give You thanks in the great assembly; I will praise You among many people."

R eading the above verse of scripture without context, you may think that David was in the midst of peace and prosperity. After all, isn't that when we sing our praises to God? Grab a Bible, or whatever electronic device you use, and read the entire chapter. You will find David wrestling with the adversity surrounding him. Yet, he is able to pause and say, *"I will praise You among many people!"*

It is fascinating, or at least interesting, that David uses the words "great" and "many" when referencing the assembly and the people. Why not just say, "I will give You thanks in the assembly and praise You among the people/congregation?"

David's words seem to also point to a future time. In Revelation 7:9-10, John writes,

> *After these things I looked, and behold, a great multitude which no one could number, of all nations, tribes, peoples, and tongues, standing before the throne and before the Lamb, clothed with white robes, with palm branches in their hands, and crying out with a loud voice, saying,*

*"Salvation belongs to our God who sits on the
throne, and to the Lamb!"*

Could it be that in the midst of crying out, *"Lord, how long
will you look on? Rescue me from their destructions,"* David
saw the end of all things? Could it be that his current question
was answered but that the ultimate solution to his problem was
yet future? We live in a time of great uncertainty, so much so
that prophecies of Messiah's imminent return are more urgent
than they've ever been.

How far beyond your circumstances do you see?

Even if David did not see what John describes in the book
of Revelation, he was speaking into an event that occurred in
the future, and it delighted him. We are much closer to that
time, and it should delight us even more. Though the winds of
distress and anxiety increase around us, the Lord is a shield surrounding us. We who are hidden in Messiah will join David in
the great assembly; we will stand among the many people who
sing praises to Adonai. Take comfort in the knowledge of Him
who is mighty to save us out of all our troubles. Sing praises to
Him who has given us great joy and peace.

Bow down before the King of glory and rejoice in the
great victory. Exalt Him who has clothed us in rich garments
and spread a table of rich delicacies before us. Walk upright
knowing that you are numbered among the great assembly and
counted among the many.

DAY 10 – GOD'S FAITHFULNESS

Psalm 36:1-6 (NKJV)

"An oracle within my heart concerning the transgression of the wicked: There is no fear of God before his eyes. For he flatters himself in his own eyes, when he finds out his iniquity and when he hates. The words of his mouth are wickedness and deceit; He has ceased to be wise and to do good. He devises wickedness on his bed; He sets himself in a way that is not good; He does not abhor evil. Your mercy, O Lord, is in the heavens; Your faithfulness reaches to the clouds. Your righteousness is like the great mountains; Your judgments are a great deep; O Lord, You preserve man and beast."

David frequently pondered the ways of wicked and prideful people and questioned why it was they seemed to thrive and increase in earthly wealth. This psalm is just one example of such ponderings. However, here we see that David is talking about intentional wickedness. This person plans wickedness while lying comfortably in bed and purposely decides to do what is not good. Even those with the discerning counsel of the Holy Spirit have difficulty understanding this type of behavior. To those without the Holy Spirit, this behavior has no plausible explanation either.

David himself apparently did not fully understand this. He said, *"Your mercy is in the heavens,"* acknowledging that this is way over his head.

The Lord declared this in Isaiah 55:9: *"As the heavens are higher than the earth, so are My ways higher than your ways, and My thoughts than your thoughts."* The Lord is merciful to the just and the unjust and, like the wheat and the tears, allows the righteous and the wicked to grow together.

In our suffering, we sometimes complain that God allows bad things to happen, exclaiming, "If He is so good, why does He allow this and that?" David said, *"Your faithfulness reaches the clouds."* It is notable to see that David did not indicate to whom God was faithful. He did not say, *"Your faithfulness to the righteous reaches the clouds."* No, God is faithful to all because He is, first of all, faithful to Himself, as there is none higher than He. Like great mountains, His righteousness cannot be moved, and like the depth of great oceans, we cannot comprehend the depth of His judgement with which He judges the earth and its inhabitants.

The Lord preserves man and beast, the just and the unjust, the faithful and the faithless, because He is love and His will is for all to come to Him for salvation; it is His will that none should perish. His mercy allows sinful people like you and me to approach His throne of grace and be cleansed from the stain of sin.

The Lord preserves man and beast, the sinner and the righteous, the tame and the wild. He feeds the birds, adorns the flowers, and leads the defenseless sheep to food and water. He says to us that the very hairs of our head are numbered and that we should not therefore fear because we are more valuable than birds and flowers.

Are you fearful and worried today? Take comfort in this: that God loves us and His desire is to save us. There is no place too high, no valley too wide, ocean too deep, that He will not be with us to save us. Take a bold step in His direction and know that His arms are wide open as He runs to embrace you.

DAY 11 – STAND FIRM

Nahum 1:7 (NKJV)

"The Lord is good, a stronghold in time of trouble;
He takes care of those who take refuge in Him."

W hen the prophet Nahum uttered these words, he was in the midst of rebuking and declaring the end of Nineveh. Can you tell? That was sort of a rhetorical question; yes, sort of. If you came upon this verse of scripture without having read the preceding verses or the verses that follow, you may think this is one of the psalms that only discusses the goodness of God.

Still, this text needs no qualifier because it is a truth that can stand alone; the Lord IS good! He is good to those who know and honor Him and to those who do not. He causes it to rain on the just and the unjust alike. The Lord IS a stronghold in the time of trouble. King Solomon adds, *"The righteous runs to Him and are safe"* (Prov. 18:10).

Local and federal governments have put in place warning systems and built designated places of refuge in the event of natural disasters. During some natural disasters that have occurred recently in the United States, we've seen what can happen when those systems fail — or when they work as designed but the warnings are ignored. Places of refuge can only serve their purposes when we enter them. Engineers design these places specifically to withstand flooding, hurricanes, earthquakes, fires, etc. They are capable of housing and sustaining far more people than our individual homes and withstanding those elements our homes fail to shelter us from.

In the reading above, Nineveh was, again, facing God's wrath. They had previously experienced His goodness when Jonah warned them to repent or God would destroy them in forty days. Like many of us, the people of Nineveh repented and may have had every intent to stay on the right path, but they slid backward into their former ways.

Where are you today? Have you experienced God's goodness but let yourself slide backward? Or have you come to depend on your own strength to save you in the time of trouble? Do not forsake what God has put in place for you. His warning systems will never fail, and His shelter is never breached.

He is who He is! God never changes, and He never shifts from one position to the next. It is we who are unstable and must act on what is there for us. The Lord is good, but we don't *have* to welcome His goodness. He is a stronghold in the time of trouble, but we don't *have* to run to Him when we experience trouble.

Today, take time to reflect on your journey with God. Assess your position and stand firm in Messiah. Do not forsake the goodness of God; run to Him and be safe. Wait patiently under His wings. *"He takes care of those who take refuge in Him."*

DAY 12 – KINDNESS AND STEADFAST LOVE

Proverbs 19:22 (CJB)

"A man's lust is his shame and a poor man is better than a liar."

Other translations render the first half of this verse, "The desire of a man is his kindness" (KJV), "What is desired in a man is kindness" (NKJV), "What is desired in a man is steadfast love" (ESV), and "What is desirable in a man is his kindness" (NASB).

Regardless of the Bible translation, the message remains the same—Kindness is better than shame, and poverty more honorable than lying lips. The Hebrew word used here for "kindness," "love," "goodness," and "steadfast love" is *Chesed* (kheh'-sed). The words "desire" and "lust" are translated from the Hebrew, *Ta'avah* (tah-av- aw'), which may be used to convey both positive and negative thought or state of being.

What is it that you desire in a friend, a wife, a husband, etc.? Do we ever hope to form a relationship with a lustful, unkind person? Do we delight in someone who tells lies and acts deceitfully? It is difficult to imagine anyone answering yes to any of these questions, which is why the next question is so important: Are you that person?

Yeshua said we should do unto others as we would have them do to us. Do you know of a liar who delights in being lied to, a thief who enjoys being robbed, or an unkind person who relishes being treated with contempt?

In this time of self-examination, it is important that we are completely honest with ourselves about those inherent sins that we become aware of. Do not try to push them off or to drown them out with excuses or rationalization. Allow the Holy Spirit to bring to the surface whatever sin or ungodly beliefs have evaded your awareness throughout your life so that He may cleanse you of them.

We are not only guilty of lying to others; we often lie to ourselves by denying the reality that we may be holding on to sinful behaviors or ungodly beliefs. We often dwell on the implications of confronting indwelling sin that may leave us exposed and vulnerable. We often lie to ourselves, telling ourselves that we are pure. This way, we do not have to confront the fact that whatever remains unconfessed sets us at odds with the Holy Spirit. However, God says that it is better to be poor than to be a liar.

Today, be honest with yourself and others also. Do not allow fear to lead you into sin. Do not look at the ramifications of your righteousness in the sight of man but look to Yeshua. *"Seek first the kingdom of God and His righteousness and all these things will be added to you"* (Matthew 6:33).

Let kindness and steadfast love be your guide. Speak the truth regardless of the potential ramifications (even poverty), and be completely honest with yourself in the process. Search your heart and walk in righteousness. God wants to do a wonderful work in each of us; will you let Him?

DAY 13 – FAITH OVER FEAR

2 Timothy 1:6-8 (NKJV)

"Therefore I remind you to stir up the gift of God which is in you through the laying on of my hands. <u>For God has not given us a spirit of fear, but of power and of love and of a sound mind.</u> Therefore do not be ashamed of the testimony of our Lord, nor of me His prisoner, but share with me in the sufferings for the gospel according to the power of God."

M any of us have used the seventh verse of this passage (underlined) to either encourage or rebuke others. Not that they are wrong, but any text used out of context loses the power that therein exists. We often do not stop to ask, "What is the gift of God that we possess?" You may have heard the phrase, "When you see a 'therefore' in Scripture, you should stop and ask what it is there for."

Paul was referring to Timothy's genuine faith when he said, "Stir up the gift of God that is in you"—faith that was passed down from his grandmother, Lois, and his mother, Eunice (2 Tim. 1:5). This may sound familiar to you, and if so, it is because Paul also referenced the gift of faith in his letter to the church in Ephesus. *"For by grace you have been saved through faith, and that not of yourselves; it is the gift of God, not of works, lest anyone should boast"* (Eph. 2:8-9).

So, how should this reshape our thinking and our approach to the world?

Fear can cripple us and prevent us from operating in the Spirit. Faith overcomes fear, and through this faith, we can operate in power, with love, and with a sound mind to be the kingdom men and women we are appointed to be in this life. We should focus less on what God has not given us and more on what He has given us—we should focus on the gift of faith, not fear.

Today is a good day to try something different—something the world will not understand, for it is contrary to worldly thinking. This is a good day to stop focusing on your fears and to begin operating in faith. Why spend time staring at the scary details of life when you can use that time to stir up the free gift of faith through the Holy Spirit? Where faith abounds, fear shrinks away. The world tells us that fear is good because it keeps us from making mistakes or that it gives us the extra energy to overcome. If God has not given us a spirit of fear, how then can it be a good thing?

"Every good gift and every perfect gift is from above, and comes down from the Father of lights" (James 1:17). God did not give us a spirit of fear; therefore, it is not a good thing, and if we have fear, it can only come from one other source, the devil. Time spent in battle against our fears is time dedicated to what is not of God. Therefore, focus on your faith and walk confidently in what God has given you with joy. Stir up the gift of faith and proclaim boldly the name of Messiah Yeshua, our King and on the kingdom of God, our heavenly Father.

DAY 14 – SPEAK WISDOM

Psalm 37:30-31 (NKJV)

"The mouth of the righteous speaks wisdom, and his tongue talks of justice. The law of his God is in his heart; none of his steps shall slide."

Meditate on this verse for a minute before reading beyond this point. What is the Lord saying to you? Are you convicted, encouraged, discouraged, or unaffected? Are the words that flow from your lips always words of wisdom?

These words from the Psalmist are not a suggestion. They put us in a difficult situation because in this broken and sinful life, it is difficult to avoid speaking foolishly. Thankfully, we have a loving Father, who is gracious to forgive us when we confess our sins and ask for forgiveness. Does this mean we needn't try to avoid foolish talk? Of course not! It means if our words *are* unrighteous or if we champion injustice, God is faithful to forgive.

The Psalmist gives us the key to speaking wisdom and using our tongues to speak up for justice; that is, we must keep the law of God on our hearts. When we stay focused on the Word of God, we keep our feet on solid ground, so we can stand firm in righteousness and justice. The law of God is good, and the outcome of holding fast to it is righteous deeds, wise words, and champions of justice.

Do you speak wisdom or folly? Do your words champion justice or injustice? If you keep the law of God in your heart, you should yearn for wisdom and justice. If you keep to His words, any act of injustice or words of condemnation should convict and lead you to repentance. We should always build and not tear down; we should free and not restrain. Our words should preserve peace and help others grow, not the other way around. Does this mean we cannot rebuke and correct? No, on the contrary, it is often through stern rebuke and correction that we grow. We are a stubborn people and often go our own ways. A rebuke received in love, a correction spoken in peace, is as fine gold to the poor.

So, whether through encouragement or praise, or even gentle correction, how can your words make a difference to someone today?

DAY 15 – GOD'S SALVATION PLAN

Job 23:10-11 (NKJV)

"But He knows the way that I take; When He has tested me, I shall come forth as gold. My foot has held fast to His steps; I have kept His way and not turned aside."

I f anyone had the law of God on his heart, it was Job. Even those who don't know the Bible very well are familiar, at least in part, with Job's story. God, in responding to Satan, described Job as blameless. How would you feel if you knew that you were blameless in God's sight? God also described David as a man after His own heart, and even when David committed grievous sins against Him, God did not change his mind or say otherwise.

At the end of Job's story, God rebuked him as one *"who darkens counsel by words without knowledge"* (Job 38:2). God rebuked David when he sinned and Job for his words spoken in ignorance. It is not far-fetched to read Job's words and think that what he said was not at all wrong. What does this all tell us? Our thoughts and ways are not God's thoughts and ways. Our righteousness is not dependent on us or our ability to live sinless, faultless lives. We can only hold fast to his law because

He gives us the ability to do so. We can only gain forgiveness because He is willing to forgive.

Job was confident that he was living a righteous life, a life that would not be shaken by testing. He was confident that his feet were firmly planted and that his life was one of pious observance of God's law. One could confidently say that Job was more confident in Who he served than in his own righteousness. This should be *our* mindset as well.

Some may argue, "Why strive to live a righteous life if our righteousness doesn't save us?" This question in itself is spoken out of ignorance because it shows a lack of awareness of God's invitation for us to participate in His plan of salvation. Additionally, this section of Job is only half the story. We will see that this was not the end of Job's life but a turning point. Job's life is a perfect example of our exile in this age. We will experience trials and tribulation, but God Himself says, "I have overcome the world." If you have answered the call—if Messiah Yeshua is your Lord and Savior—you too have overcome the world because we are in Him and He is in us.

God has *"raised us up together, and made us sit together in the heavenly places in Messiah Yeshua, that in the ages to come He might show the exceeding riches of His grace in His kindness toward us in Messiah Yeshua"* (Eph. 2:6-7).

How will you participate in God's salvation plan today? God knows the way you take. If He tested you today, would you come out as fine gold? Have your feet held fast to His steps, and have you kept His ways without turning aside? Whatever your answer, remember that it is His righteousness through Messiah that saves us. So, I ask again, how will you participate in God's salvation plan today?

DAY 16 – LONG LIFE

Psalm 39:4, 11 (NKJV)

"Lord, make me to know my end and what is the measure of my days, that I may know how frail I am. When with rebukes You correct man for iniquity, You make his beauty melt away like a moth; surely every man is vapor."

We marvel at people who live to and beyond ninety years of age, especially if they are still mobile and independent. Yet, the Psalmist says that our days are few and vanish like vapor. It was Job who said, *"Man who is born of woman is of few days and full of trouble. He comes forth like a flower and fades away. He flees like a shadow and does not continue"* (Job 14:1-2).

We often consider our future and all the marvelous accomplishments we have ahead of us. The world tells us that we must develop a five-year to ten-year plan, all focused on where we see ourselves in our careers, savings, family, etc. Contrast this to what David said in Psalm 39:4. He was not asking to know his end because he needed to make sure he accomplished all his goals and dreams. David knew that no matter how long he lived, it would still be short in God's sight.

"Surely every man is vapor!" Consider how much time passes before vapor completely vanishes from existence. Now

put that in perspective with life and think about how you could live differently considering the brevity of our existence.

God promises that a life lived for Him and according to His will shall continue with Him into eternity. He also warns us that without Him, life is full of iniquity and will be cut off. David reminded himself of just how frail and short life is. It was a reminder for him to live a life free of iniquity. So too should we remind ourselves to walk this life in righteousness. The troubles we experience in life seem to last forever, and the good times seem to pass ever so quickly. Yet, it is all a brief moment in God's sight. Take care to guard your ways in good times and bad times because it all passes like vapor, and then we enter into eternity. Live a life dedicated to God so that your place in eternity will be one of peace, not torment.

DAY 17 – FULL OBEDIENCE

Deuteronomy 6:6-7 (NKJV)

"And these words which I command you today shall be in your heart. You shall teach them diligently to your children, and shall talk of them when you sit in your house, when you walk by the way, when you lie down, and when you rise up."

God gives us many commands in the Bible, and while we often focus much on the Ten Commandments, the others are no less important. It is possible the we have focused so narrowly on the commands that we fail to obey the command to observe the commands. By that, I mean that we fail to recognize and obey the command to teach the commandments diligently to our children; we often fail to discuss them in our homes, or when we go about our way; we don't often meditate on them when we go to sleep, and they may not be the first things on our minds when we wake up. Yet, all these are God's commands to us.

Many have argued that the reason we have such chaos in society today is that parents are failing to teach their children at home. Some say it is what they are being taught at home that is the source of the problem. While both arguments may be valid, believers should remember that the Bible is the true source of inspiration and the standard by which we are to raise up a child. Without godly counsel, our children will go the way of the world; even with godly counsel, they may still go the way of the world, but the seed of faith that parents plant from an early age can still spring forth at some point in a child's life to bring about repentance and good fruit.

Today, if you have not considered and obeyed God's command to obey His commands, start doing so. Yesterday has already passed, but today brings about a fresh opportunity to get it right. Read the Word with a keen eye for God's every command and a heart that is desperate to obey each one. Instead of focusing so narrowly on the command itself, broaden your focus to see the command and the instructions surrounding it. The Lord desires obedience more than sacrifice (1 Sam. 15:22). We cannot obey in part; obedience must be in full. Partial obedience is disobedience; therefore, obey in full.

DAY 18 – SPIRITUAL MATURITY

1 Corinthians 13:11 (NKJV)

"When I was a child, I spoke as a child, I under-
stood as a child, I thought as a child; but when
I became a man, I put away childish things."

When you look back at your childhood, as much of it as you can remember, do you ever wonder why in the world you did some of the things you did? Or did you have perfect knowledge and behave in a perfect way? Do you find yourself acting in a way or saying the things your parents/guardians did and said to you when you were a teenager?

Our life's journey is one of constant learning and maturing in knowledge and understanding. Our thoughts and behaviors change with the ever-expanding knowledge we acquire through our experiences and encounters. Sometimes, we become firmer in what we believe, and at other times, we change our approach based on a developed understanding.

The same is true for our spiritual growth. As we study the Bible, worship with the brethren, participate in small groups, and listen to biblical exegetes from reputable teachers, we mature spiritually. If you are not maturing in your faith, you should examine closely the reason. What part of your faith are you not nurturing? How often do you study the Word—not just read a verse or two? Do you attend church/congregation regularly? Do you participate in small groups?

Newsflash! As we grow and mature, we change our approach to life. This is just a natural part of life that can only be avoided if we lock ourselves away without any interaction or study. This should also be the case for our spiritual growth. All believers should participate in things biblical, with other members of the body of Messiah, and more frequently than we engage the world.

If we engage the world, we will mature in ways of the world; if we engage the Word, we will mature in the Word. It is a balancing act on a beam that must tilt more toward the Word of God. Yeshua said, *"You are not of the world, but I chose you out of the world, therefore the world hates you"* (John 15:18b). A world that hates us will lead us astray because we do not conform to its ways. Therefore, mature in the ways of God by engaging in the Word of God. The apostle John also said, *"Do not love the world or the things in the world. If anyone loves the world, the love of the Father is not in him"* (1 John 2:15-18).

Today, make a careful observation of your spiritual maturity and what you do to mature in your faith. Develop a strategy to either focus more on your spiritual maturity or to maintain your current rate of maturity, making sure your spiritual maturity far outpaces that of the world.

DAY 19 – GOD SUSTAINS YOU

Psalm 40:1-3 (CJB)

"How blessed are those who care for the poor!
When calamity comes, Adonai will save them.
Adonai will preserve them, keep them alive, and
make them happy in the land. You will not hand
them over to the whims of their enemies. Adonai
sustains them on their sickbed; when they lie ill,
you make them recover."

There is a source from which everything flows. Those who come against you do so because they are rooted in the enemy of your soul, whose ultimate goal is to destroy you. To the first verse of this Psalm, you could add, "…care for the stranger, the destitute, the needy, the sick, the grieving, the diseased, etc." The Lord said it is a blessing to us when we care for those in need, without regard for ourselves. He promises to care for our needs in the process.

Did you notice that He did not say we would not get sick or experience difficulties in life? No, He said that He would sustain us in times of sickness and make us recover; the blessing is in His presence and our recovery. When you are experiencing difficulties, know that God is in it with you to sustain and deliver you. It is often difficult to focus beyond our pain and discomfort to see that God has not abandoned us, but the reality is, He is always right there with us.

In the midst of Job's suffering, his wife asked him, *"Why do you still hold on to your integrity? Curse God and die"* (Job 2:9). A pastor once lauded Job's wife, saying that it was because of her compassion and love for Job that she said that. However, what Job's wife missed in that moment was that God was protecting and sustaining Job. Satan wanted to kill Job, but God did not give him that authority. If his wife truly wanted to help, she should have encouraged him to trust God's plan, despite the pain.

Satan does not want you to remain faithful to God and would be delighted to watch us curse God and die, but God still holds our lives in His hands. Yeshua holds the keys of life and death, and His desire is to give life. Though you suffer sickness, loss, poverty, and all kinds of ills in this life, God is with you through it and will lift you up at the set time.

Today, give God thanks for His great mercies toward you and walk about with confidence that He has not abandoned you but that He is always with you.

DAY 20 – HOLD FAST

2 Timothy 1:13-14 (NKJV)

"Hold fast the pattern of sound words which you have heard from me, in faith and love which are in Christ Jesus. That good thing which was committed to you, keep by the Holy Spirit who dwells in us."

W e are a generation of people who like to repeat what we consider great quotes from famous or influential people. If you walk the streets of Washington, DC, you will not lack an opportunity to read a quote. We repeat them in speeches, books, movies, and the like. Sometimes, repeating them even makes us think ourselves wise, or it may give that impression.

Paul tells Timothy to hold fast to the sound words which he (Timothy) learned from him. No one would consider the apostle Paul a man of few words. In fact, in Acts 20:9, we learn about Eutychus, who fell asleep and consequently fell from the window of a second-floor room where Paul's teaching went on and on. But what was Paul telling Timothy? To draw on some really good quotes to lift his spirits or others? Not at all!

Paul goes on to describe his words as "that good thing," meaning the Gospel. He was telling Timothy to live according to the Gospel of Messiah Yeshua, with the help of the Ruach Ha'Kodesh (Holy Spirit), who dwells in him. Sure, the Gospel makes for good quotes, which we believers are very much guilty of overusing, misusing, and/or abusing, but we should use them. Moreover, we must also live by them, through the Holy Spirit, in whole, not in part.

It is good and encouraging to read a daily verse or passage of scripture. It is even better to read the whole chapter, so as to have the larger context of the message and maybe even a devotional to go along with it. It is just as good and encouraging to live out the Gospel. That is what Paul means in the words "hold fast." Let the Word penetrate you and flow through you in your thoughts, words, and actions. To hold fast to the Gospel is to hold fast the Messiah Yeshua, the Word made flesh. Live as Messiah did, with faith and love, and the Holy Spirit will keep you, strengthen you, and light your path every step of the way.

DAY 21 – FORGIVENESS

Matthew 6:14-15 (NASB)

"For if you forgive others their offenses, your heavenly Father will also forgive you; but if you do not forgive others their offenses, your heavenly Father will not forgive yours."

Forgiveness is a reciprocal act meant to lighten our burdens and give us peace. Even if a person against whom you have sinned doesn't offer their forgiveness, you still receive forgiveness from God. It is an act that always rewards, and it is a reward that is life-giving.

Unforgiveness, on the other hand, is a burden that eats away at our very souls. First and foremost, when we don't forgive others, God does not forgive us, even if we receive forgiveness from someone we have offended. His actions are not based on what others do toward us but our relationship with Him. Additionally, the anger, hurt, and other emotions we experience when others cause offense is a burdensome load that manifests with each memory of that event.

Forgiveness allows us to remember but not carry the load, because God has taken it off our backs. You may often hear the phrase, "Leave it at the cross." Yeshua has borne the burden, and forgiveness is now in the asking. The sacrifice is always provided once for all and for all time.

Are you holding on to an offense? How is it of any benefit to you? What emotions rise to the surface when you think of it? Unforgiveness is an open window for the enemy to climb through to wreak havoc on your spiritual life. It is a way for the devil to exploit our vulnerabilities and bring an accusation against us. Don't give the enemy any ammunition to use against you; close the breach and deny him entry.

Understand that forgiveness is not for the offender's sake. In fact, the offender doesn't even need to know you've forgiven. This is particularly important in a case of abuse or crime. However, forgiveness is relinquishing the right to punish or judge another and leaving that right to God. Forgiving someone who has offended you frees you from a responsibility that was never yours to carry.

Forgive so that you may attain forgiveness, peace, and justice. Whatever others have done to you cannot be undone but can be rectified, and the Lord has promised to repay. So, give it to God with faith that He knows just what to do and only He has the power to do it. The rewards of forgiveness are eternally good; take hold of it.

DAY 22 – DRESS FOR ACTION

Matthew 3:1-6 (ESV)

*"In those days John the Baptist came preaching
in the wilderness of Judea, 'Repent, for the
kingdom of heaven is at hand.' For this is he
who was spoken of by the prophet Isaiah when
he said, 'The voice of one crying in the wilderness: "Prepare the way of the Lord; make
his paths straight."' Now John wore a garment
of camel's hair and a leather belt around his
waist, and his food was locusts and wild honey.
Then Jerusalem and all Judea and all the region
about the Jordan were going out to him, and
they were baptized by him in the river Jordan,
confessing their sins."*

Many have wondered about the significance of writing about John's attire in this chapter of Matthew's gospel. Some have preached sermons on it, and many conjectures are offered, but its true purpose may yet remain somewhat shrouded. This we can be sure of: John must have been one uncomfortable man! Beyond his clothing was a message that attracted many, including the ruling class of his day. It may not be too far-fetched to say that he would have been labeled men-tally ill and dangerous in today's culture, especially in the West.

Yet, he was a man elected of God to blaze a trail for the Messiah, and blaze the trail he did. His message was fiery, controversial, and offensive, even for those of his time. Still, he attracted those who considered themselves experts in the law.

Many of us have come to expect the Gospel of Yeshua to be delivered in a nice pretty package by a person dressed in the most fashionable attire. We tend to give our attention to those who make us feel good about ourselves and whose personality could charm a rattlesnake. This may or may not apply to you, but a good self-examination is never a bad idea.

John was carrying out the mission/ministry to which he was called, without regard to what others thought. He purposely lived a sacrificial life without dependence on others and in such a way as to humbly leave his needs in the hands of God—his clothes, his food, and even his dwelling place.

Are you dressed for action? Today is a good day to take a close look at how faithful you have been in the ministry God has called you to and to whom you have been most accountable. Those around us often offer their "good" advice, even when they are not fulfilling their own calling, or they may have a completely different set of gifts and calling from you.

Take it up with God today. Seek His thoughts and direction and commit yourself to walking in the way that He prepared for you. Blaze the trail for Messiah and live the sacrificial life believers are called to with all humility, faith, and grace. Yeshua died so that we have life. He is alive, and His Spirit dwells in us.

Live for Him!

DAY 23 – BELIEF AND UNBELIEF

Psalm 44:1 (NKJV)

"We have heard with our ears, O God, our fathers have told us the deeds You did in their days, in days of old."

Many who question the accuracy of the Bible often use the excuse that it was written by men who were prone to error and exaggeration. Setting aside the fact that they completely miss or don't understand the God factor, there is often an air of hypocrisy in these excuses.

History is man's retelling of past occurrences, and we take pride in that which applies to us, our families, and our nations. We teach it diligently to our children in both formal and informal settings, often treating it as inherent. So, why do we accept the traditions and written events of man but question those of God? How much do you question the stories your parents and grandparents told you growing up?

God does not have to give us proof of His existence or prove that what is written in His words is true, but He understands our frail nature and does so anyway. Archeological discoveries and prophetic fulfillment bears witness to the accuracy of the Bible. Many still arrive at fanciful excuses not to believe, but like Pharaoh, a hardened heart hides what is revealed to it. The writer of the letter to the Hebrews referenced a cloud of witnesses in Hebrews 12:1. The Psalmist above is also talking about the same witnesses—previous generations who witnessed the miraculous works of God and who passed them down from one generation to the other.

What about you? What is your view of the Bible? Do you believe that the Bible is the inerrant Word of God, written down by men through the inspiration of His Holy Spirit? Or, like so many today, believe that it is good moral teaching but that it is simply the work of men? If you believe the latter, I encourage you to test it and see. Study it carefully and search out what you have read to see if it does not hold up to your scrutiny. If you already believe, keep on believing, learning, practicing, and teaching so that you may excel in what God has prepared in advance for you.

DAY 24 – ALL
THINGS FOR GOOD

Romans 8:28 (NKJV)

"And we know that all things work together for good, to those who love God, to those who are called according to His purpose."

This is one of the most quoted texts in the New Testament and for good reason—it is true! God takes every trial and turns it into victory and every disappointment into an opportunity. Still, there is much more to be said of this verse. It is essential that we examine the 'and' at the beginning of the sentence. Ancient Hebrew did not have punctuation marks, nor did the text contain chapter and verse numbers.

In Romans 8:27, Paul writes, *"Now He who searches the hearts knows what the mind of the Spirit is, because He makes intercession for the saints according to the will of God."* Keeping this in mind, we must hold the truth of verse 28 with the recognition that God searches our hearts and knows our intentions. He sees our tomorrow as if it has already happened; in fact, to Him, it *has* already happened. Therefore, while God does work all things for good, we must enter every situation with a clear conscience and a heart that longs for Him and His purposes.

Psalm 37:23-24 says, *"The steps of a good man are ordered by the Lord and He delight in his way. Though he fall, he shall not be utterly cast down, for the Lord upholds him with His hands."* This psalm speaks truth to Romans 8:28 by making it clear that it is the Lord who directs the steps of a good person. God delights in our good works and all that honors Him. Both Romans 8:28 and Psalm 37:24 tell us that God will uphold us in times of trouble; that when we fall, He will lift us up and deliver us; and that through trial, He refines us and makes us purer.

This is all possible because it is God who does it. It is He who upholds us when we stumble, and it is He who guides us. Messiah Yeshua makes intercession for us to save us. We must endeavor to keep our thoughts and actions pure so as to deny others a chance to accuse us.

DAY 25 – QUALITIES OF MESSIAH

2 Peter 1:3, 5-6 (NASB)

"Seeing that His divine power has granted to us everything pertaining to life and godliness, through the true knowledge of Him who called us by His own glory and excellence. Now for this very reason also, applying all diligence, in your faith supply moral excellence, and in your moral excellence, knowledge, and in your knowledge, self-control, and in your self-control, perseverance, and in your perseverance, godliness, and in your godliness, brotherly kindness, and in your brotherly kindness, love."

Moral excellence, knowledge, self-control, perseverance, godliness, brotherly kindness, and love. These seven qualities, according to the apostle Peter, are qualities of Messiah's followers, and in living by them, we can be sure no one can render us useless nor unfruitful in the true knowledge of Messiah Yeshua. Peter goes on to say that those who lack these qualities are either blind or short-sighted, having forgotten their former purification (2 Peter 1:9-10).

Have you ever been accused of having changed? If you have, was it for better or worse? Once we become believers, having accepted Yeshua as our Lord and Savior, we are to look, think, speak, and act differently from those in the world and even our former selves. The Epistles were written to churches. Peter was encouraging the church to keep these qualities in mind, knowing that in operating in them, they will be fruitful for the kingdom—they will grow in the true knowledge of Messiah.

There is a warning here also. If we do not possess all seven traits, it is time for a thorough self-examination. We should also be willing to accept correction from the brethren without offense. If, indeed, without these qualities we are truly blind or short sighted, recognizing our shortcomings may not be so easy. It is for this reason shared accountability is so critical.

Today, examine your own heart. Take this matter to the Lord and even ask a friend if you demonstrate these qualities and whether you demonstrate them consistently. Whether you have an active ministry or not, Peter says that by possessing these seven qualities, we will be fruitful and will grow in the true knowledge of Messiah Yeshua.

DAY 26 – THE STRONG HAND OF GOD

Isaiah 54:17 (NKJV)

"'No weapon formed against you shall prosper, and every tongue which rises against you in judgment You shall condemn. This is the heritage of the servants of the Lord, and their righteousness is from Me,' says the Lord."

W hy does it so often feel as if the weapons formed against us do prosper and our troubles often never cease? The reality is that we have an enemy who is persistent, resourceful, and cunning. He will throw everything at us to overwhelm us and make us feel defeated, but *"God is our refuge and strength, a very present help in trouble"* (Psalm 46:1). You may ask, "If God is my refuge, why does so much trouble come my way?" In answering, consider how a military enemy force that is outgunned can force opposing troops to run for cover. Their weapons, though inferior, are just as deadly.

God didn't say no weapon will be formed against us. No, He said the weapons formed will not prosper because HE is our refuge. He is our bunker in the event of a nuclear strike, our foxhole when rounds come downrange, our camouflage when the enemy seeks us out, and our shelter from the tempests of life.

Therefore, He says, *"Be still and know that I am God"* (Psalm 46:10). Be still and know the power and glory of God will shatter into pieces those weapons that come against you. Be still and watch Him scatter the troops that charge toward you. Be still and know that the Lord your God is your refuge and strong tower. He will not leave you desolate but will rescue you.

What is it that troubles you today, and what has taken your attention captive? The Lord says fear not, for He has overcome all these things on your behalf. Persevere in the face of resistance and recognize the strong hand of God guiding you through it all. Though darkness surrounds us, His light shines through. Even a lamp is sufficient to light our path when our hope anchors on Messiah Yeshua. Be still my heart, for He who made you knows your longings and delights in you.

DAY 27 – BEYOND APPEARANCE

Colossians 3:12 (CJB)

"Therefore, as God's chosen people, holy and dearly loved, clothe yourselves with feelings of compassion and with kindness, humility, gentleness and patience."

How do you see other people, especially people who look and act differently than you do? What is the first thing that comes to mind when you see someone you consider good looking or not so good looking? How do you react to someone who does not "fit" well within the expectations you have come to embody?

Scripture tells us we who have been baptized in Messiah have the mind of Messiah. Yeshua is the perfect embodiment of compassion, kindness, humility, gentleness, and patience. Isaiah describes the Messiah as *"One who would not snap off a broken reed or put out a smoldering candle"* (Isa. 42:3). How many of us could say that about ourselves or have another person say that about us? No doubt you may say that we are not perfect, and you are right to say so, but Messiah in us is perfect and we should endeavor to walk, think, and act as one who has the mind of Messiah Yeshua.

This is a broken and often loveless world with much cruelty being levied against the innocent in every corner of the earth. We are commissioned to be a much-needed light in today's dark world. The divisions we see in almost all corners of the earth send a dismal message of where we are going as a people. Still, we are called to clothe ourselves in love because we are children of the Author of love.

Believers are called to see beyond appearance and even personality to see the heart, longings, and the love of the Father in and for others. May this never be too high a calling.

DAY 28 – THE ADVOCATE

Proverbs 31:8-9 (CJB)

"Speak up for those who can't speak for themselves, for the rights of all who need an advocate. Speak up, judge righteously, defend the cause of the poor and the needy."

The world is not short of those who advocate for the poor, the needy, and for those who cannot speak for themselves. Many government bodies and private entities have put into place programs that assist those whose voices are often silenced and whose needs might otherwise go unmet. Many institutions offer pro-bono work, donations, and structured volunteer programs that care for the disadvantaged.

Still, evil seems to cast its shadow over these efforts, making them seemingly ineffective at times. Some people take advantage of these programs for their own benefit, both as provider and consumer. Benefactors of these heart-led efforts may even act as if there is not enough being done to meet their needs. Additionally, sometimes well-meaning efforts fail due to the lack of sufficient donations of time, talent, and treasure to make them sustainable.

One can confidently say that because God calls for advocacy—for the defense of the weak, the poor, and the needy—Satan will attack any such efforts. For this reason, we must be even more vigilant and steadfast in such works. Whenever we step out in faith, the possibility of resistance is increased two-fold. Therefore, we must be securely connected to God through His Holy Spirit; we must always don the full armor of God.

No amount of good work can change the trajectory of this world. What is written must be accomplished because God's Word will never return to Him void (Isa. 55:11). One needn't read to the end of the Bible to know that this world has a definite end, for the prophets have long foretold what will happen. What the apostle John wrote in the book of Revelation describes the hope of the righteous and a way of escape for repentant sinners.

Only God can save us, but He has, in the interim, appointed us to be agents for the good of those in need. He has granted us the opportunity to be participants in His work of redemption by commissioning us to advocate for the less fortunate. While you don't have to know Messiah to do good works and to advocate for others, those whose works are grounded in Him will withstand the corruption of sin. Only what is built on Messiah, our solid Rock, will stand against the waves of the evil one, who seeks to desecrate all that is holy.

Today, be a voice for the speechless, arms for the handicap, feet for the crippled, eyes for the blind, and a source of strength for the weak. Do your work in the strength and power of the Holy Spirit and stand strong in the Rock of our salvation!

DAY 29 – TEMPTATION

James 1:2-4 (NASB)

"Regard it all as joy, my brothers, when you face various kinds of temptations; for you know that the testing of your trust produces perseverance. But let perseverance do its complete work; so that you may be complete and whole, lacking in nothing."

There lies in us the ability to learn and to put what is learned into action, if we so choose. We often hear the common phrase, "Learn from your mistakes," and we should absolutely learn from them. However, new knowledge is only as effective as much as it is put into practice. Only then can we transform information into real energy to produce results that we can improve upon over time.

You may be one of the many who often pray to avoid temptation, but it is not temptation that we should be most concerned about. Temptation, though unpleasant and uncomfortable, is not itself sin but can lead to sin. James tells us that through temptation, we learn patience and perseverance. For that reason, he said to take joy in the temptation (James 1:2). We run a better race when we practice and push beyond physical and mental obstacles to realize the full potential of our bodies.

Temptation helps us to realize the limitations of our own strength, the point at which we must ask the Lord to help us or we may fall into sin. It is in the face of temptation and testing that we mature in faith and become more confident—not confidence in ourselves but in the One who can deliver us from sin and who strengthens us to overcome.

Yeshua told Peter that Satan requested to sift him as wheat but added that He prayed for Peter that his faith would not fail him and that when he returns, he will strengthen his brethren (Luke 22:31-34). Yeshua could have said no to Satan's request, but He did not—the same way that God did not say no to Satan's request to test Job. Yeshua knew that the sifting would make Peter stronger in his faith and, once victorious, Peter would be a source of strength to his brethren.

Never having to face temptation is a sweet longing for the child of God, but we know that in this life, temptation will come. So, while we keep our eyes on the day when all will be fulfilled, we must face reality with courage and full confidence that our heavenly Father will not let us fall.

If we never mature in our faith or grow in the knowledge of our Lord and Savior, Messiah Yeshua, we will remain susceptible to the enemy's attacks and will be of little use to those around us who are undergoing their own assaults. Put your knowledge into action so that it may blossom and bear much fruit for the kingdom of God. Instead of praying never to fall into temptation, pray for God to deliver you from it and teach you how to use your experience to mature and become one who teaches others to do the same.

DAY 30 – RANSOMED

Psalm 49:7-10 (ESV)

"Truly no man can ransom another, or give to God the price of his life, for the ransom of their life is costly and can never suffice, that he should live on forever and never see the pit. For he sees that even the wise die; the fool and the stupid alike must perish and leave their wealth to others."

This Psalm passage offers a new perspective to the notion of *"eye for an eye,"* which, in practice, would only leave two people partially blind. Consider the word "ransom." The purpose of a ransom is to provide a benefit to both parties, regardless of how the need for a ransom came about. The first thought that comes to mind when we hear the word "ransom" is payment to release someone or something from captivity, which is also how the Merriam-Webster dictionary defines it.

This world was taken captive when Adam and Eve made the grave mistake of falling for Satan's deception in the Garden of Eden. Their error and ours brought about death, which demands a reckoning. Only life can redeem life, and only one life could make that ransom permanent. Messiah Yeshua is the only permanent solution to our state of sinfulness, for in this fallen world, our sins continue to manifest, and we continually fall for the same lies and deceits of the devil.

God Himself ransomed us from the grip of sin and death. He made a way for us by sending His Son to die once for all time so that our past, present, and future sins may be cleansed in His blood. We should always endeavor to live sinless lives, to leave behind those things that displease God, and to serve Him only. We know that in this fallen world, full of temptations and all manner of evil, we run the risk of falling into sin at every corner. But Messiah says that if we repent, He will forgive us.

One more thing: Do not walk with a guilty conscience after your sins are forgiven through Yeshua's death that washes away all guilt and shame. Repent and move on so that your ministry and your encounters can flourish for the glory of God. The price of ransom is already paid, and none other could match its worth.

Today, realize that you are a ransomed commodity priced beyond any rare gem this world could produce. Your life was worth the life of God Himself. That is how much He values us—He set aside His glory and walked among men in the dust and filth we brought on ourselves. Take pleasure in Him and not in yourself, your wealth, your possessions, or even your posterity. Treasure the love He has for you and live a life that demonstrates your true value—the value of a child of the Most High King.

DAY 31 – OBEY THE LAW

Deuteronomy 29:9 (NKJV)

*"Therefore keep the words of this covenant, and
do them, that you may prosper in all that you do."*

Many of the laws that govern a nation or localities within a nation exist for our benefit. They are meant to keep us safe, to protect us from people, things, and even ourselves. Laws that govern the roads help restrain our daredevil instincts that may endanger others. Laws that govern companies help protect us from becoming victims of unsafe practices or corporate greed.

For the most part, if we abide by the established rules, we could avoid the negative consequences from which they are intended to protect us. Conversely, there are consequences for breaking these laws, consequences that are often harsh enough to deter our worst instincts. A nation's laws apply to everyone who sets foot on or operates within its boundaries, regardless of where they hold citizenship. Similarly, local laws apply to all who tarry, pass through, or conduct business in a province where they do not live.

The Bible is our instruction manual for life. It is written for everyone, not just for Christians and Jews. It was given to the people of Israel for the benefit of the entire world, that if we abide by the laws written therein, we will prosper in all that we do. No one is exempt from the Word of God. We are all citizens of the world because the One who created us and set us in it is the Creator and Ruler of it all; He has no boundaries. As the Psalmist says, *"The earth is the LORD's, and all its fullness, the world and those who dwell therein."* (Psalm 24:1).

Because of our inherent sense of entitlement, we often do not adhere to the laws that govern the land and its inhabitants. We would be hard-pressed to find an individual who has perfectly kept the laws of man. How much more difficult would it be to find someone who has perfectly kept the laws of God? There has only been one person in the history of mankind: Messiah Yeshua.

God knows that we cannot keep His laws perfectly, so He Himself stepped into His creation in the person of Yeshua to keep them and to pay the cost of our breaking them. This was so that we can have the debt we incur wiped clean for all time. There is no judge on earth today who can would wipe away your debts from the past, present, and future, but the Judge of heaven and earth has.

He tells us to abide by His law—keep His commandments and abide in Him—but, should we fall short, His sacrifice covers the debt and we can continue in His good graces through repentance.

Don't let the burden of your iniquities keep you from walking in the freedom you have through Messiah Yeshua. Walk in faith according to the Word of God and hold fast to His commandments, but remember that *"all have sinned and fall short of the glory of God"* (Rom. 3:23). Confess your sins, ask the Lord for forgiveness, and endeavor to not repeat them. The debt has already been paid, and the Lord will not hold you liable. Prosper in His ways by holding fast to Him. Live in obedience to His Word and have assurance that His judgement of you will be your reward.

DAY 32 – BROKEN HEART

Ezekiel 6:8-9 (CJB)

"Nevertheless, I will leave a remnant, some who will escape the sword among the nations, when you have been scattered throughout the countries. Those of you who escape will remember me among the nations where they have been exiled. How broken I have been over their whoring hearts that left me, and over their eyes that went whoring after their idols! They are going to loathe themselves for all the evils they committed in their disgusting practices."

I f you have ever had your heart broken, you may know the thoughts that go through one's mind as those hurt feelings penetrate one's entire being. Jealousy can bring about some truly astonishing thoughts and acts, which would make us wonder about people's inability to operate in the "evolved" mindset we so desperately portray in superhero/super villain comics and movies. Then again, perhaps you are one of the rare people who never fantasize about having super powers. Ok, moving on!

Many consider God in the Old Testament as an angry God and use scriptures such as the ones above to support their position. What they tend to miss is the heart of God, expressed through His holiness—holiness that requires that He judge sin for what it is.

God said, *"How broken I have been over their whoring hearts that left me"* (Ezek. 6:7-9). The New King James Version says, *"I was crushed by their adulterous heart which has departed from Me."* God tells the Hebrews that He is a Jealous God, and we see His jealousy very clearly in these words. His heart is crushed by our sins and by our whoring after other gods.

In His love, God allowed a remnant of the Hebrews to remain, and in His love, He does the same for you and me. We too crush His heart when we go "whoring after idols." Yes, we still have idols! They may not be carved out of wood or stone, but they are very real. Idols are those things that take His place in our hearts.

Are there idols in your life that need to be removed in order to keep God first? Idols come in all sizes, shapes, and forms, ranging from our favorite sport teams, our toys, relationships, and yes, even carved images. Today is a good day to examine your heart to see if there is room enough for God alone. In other words, we must remove all others from the throne of our hearts so that God can take His rightful position there. For He says, *"My glory I will not give to another, nor My praise to carved images"* (Isa. 42:8).

God is jealous over you. He wants you all to Himself and can do no less than give His all to you. His love for you is perfect, and His desire for you is pure and clean. He is righteous, just, and trustworthy. He is a wise groom with the power to do above and beyond all that you can ask or imagine. Will you not take His outstretched arms today?

DAY 33 – WORD OF LIFE

Psalm 50:14-16 (NKJV)

*"'Offer to God thanksgiving, and pay your vows
to the Most High. Call upon Me in the day of
trouble; I will deliver you, and you shall glorify
Me.' But to the wicked God says: 'What right
have you to declare My statutes, or take My covenant in your mouth, seeing you hate instruction
and cast My words behind you?'"*

We love to repeat a proverb—wise sayings that make us
appear learned or that bolster our message and image.
The Bible is an oft-quoted book by people across many cultures
and nationalities. Those who argue against the need for and
the existence of God often try to throw scripture in the face of
believers when they see an opportunity for criticism.

God says to these, *"What right have you to declare My
Statutes?"* (Psalm 50:16). His words are not throw-away lines
for us to use to our benefit when we determine they are appro-
priate. They are words of life from the Author of life and are
for leading us in righteousness.

God makes many promises in Scripture, and He will be true
to fulfill each one. We can be guilty of trying to hold God to His
promises while failing to obey His commands. The Psalmist
writes that we should *"offer to God thanksgiving and pay our
vows to the Most High"* (Psalm 50:14). This is not merely a

suggestion; it is a command. Like all the other commands, we have free will to obey or ignore this one, but by choosing the latter, we are disobedient and become partakers with the wicked.

When we are obedient to God's commands, He responds to our plea for help in our day of trouble. When we make it a habit to call upon God, we offer constant praise, and we glorify Him in the process, not just in the time of trouble. He is glorified when we look to Him in good times and in difficult situations. He is glorified when we seek Him for direction in simple matters and in complex situations. He is glorified when we seek Him. Seek God, and He will answer!

DAY 34 – GOD ANSWERS

Psalm 86:1-2, 6-7 (NKJV)

"Bow down Your ear, O LORD, hear me, for I am poor and needy. Preserve my life, for I am holy; You are my God. Give ear, O LORD, to my prayer; and attend to the voice of my supplications. In the day of my trouble I will call on You, for You will answer me."

God promises to answer when we call upon Him, and the Psalmist took Him up on that offer. But first, he recognized and declared his need for God, his holiness, his righteousness, and his need to praise God. The Psalmist gives glory to God in the midst of his plea for help. He trusted that God will answer him because it is what He has promised to do.

It is often our nature to be skeptical, but faith has no place for skepticism. Faith in God is a 100 percent trust that He will do what He has said He will do. On the other hand, it is we humans who often don't do what we promise to do. Our skepticism, therefore, is often a result of our own failure to fulfill our vows. It is impossible to say we have faith when we are unfaithful to God and others.

"Preserve my life, for I am holy; You are my God!" This is a statement of confidence that the Psalmist is living in accordance with God's will, holding fast to His commandments and setting himself apart for God's purposes. He is living in obedience to

God's command to the people of Israel. *"For I am the LORD your God. You shall therefore consecrate yourselves, and you shall be holy; for I am holy"* (Lev. 11:44).

God says, *"I am your God,"* and the Psalmist said, *"You are my God."* God says, *"You shall be holy";* the Psalmist said, *"I am holy."* God says, *"Call upon me in the day of trouble";* the Psalmist says, *"I will call upon you in the day of trouble."* He is repeating God's words to Him and saying, "You have ordained, and I have kept all these statutes. Therefore, I am coming to You in confidence that You will be faithful to keep them, for You are a holy God."

What about you? Do you try to hold God to His promises in confidence that you have first lived in accordance with His will? Can you confidently say, "Answer me, for I am holy; I have been faithful to You and to Your commandments"?

To be holy does not mean that you have been perfect in all that you do or that you have never fallen short. This is not the issue at hand; the issue is whether your primary focus has been to live according to God's will; it is whether He is preeminent in your life. More importantly, this is about God's faithfulness to us and His desire to save us.

Call upon God today and do not be afraid to declare His statutes to Him. He knows what He said and will not be taken aback by your boldness. If we cannot say in conference, "I am holy," it just means there is that much more we have to ask for. It is an opportunity to acknowledge just how poor and needy you are and to acknowledge your need to glorify God and your desire of Him.

DAY 35 – HOSANNA!

Matthew 21:9 (NASB)

"The crowds going ahead of Him, and those who followed, were shouting, 'Hosanna to the Son of David; Blessed is He who comes in the name of the Lord; Hosanna in the highest!'"

The word "Hosanna" is translated *Please deliver (save) now* and is so rendered in the Complete Jewish Bible (CJB). It is often said that Israel missed the appearance of her Messiah. This passage of Scripture shows that not all (but a great majority of them) accepted Yeshua, even after this event. This is why He declared to them,

> *How often would I have gathered your children together as a hen gathers her brood under her wings, and you were not willing! Behold, your house is forsaken. And I tell you, you will not see me until you say, "Blessed is he who comes in the name of the Lord."*
>
> Luke 13:34-35

A large crowd of people had just welcomed Yeshua to Jerusalem with that very shout— *"Baruch haba b'shem Adonai!"*

Yet, Yeshua said that they will not see Him again until they make that very proclamation.

Will that be the case when He returns? Will your house be left desolate because you are not willing to be gathered to Him? Will your cry of "Hosanna" be in vain because you refuse to believe in the name of Yeshua? It happened once, and it will happen again, for many who cry, "Lord, save us," are not living in accordance with His will. We cry, "Save us," when we have no more options, effectively making God our last option instead of our first.

Make God the preeminent option in your life, that you don't have to cry, *"Hosanna,"* but with confidence that if you have to cry out, He will answer you and will save you. Praise Him daily by shouting, *"Baruch haba b'shem Adonai"* — Blessed is He who comes in the name of the Lord! Do not be ashamed to praise His name or be hesitant to bewail your need of Him. He is standing at the door of our hearts, ready to enter in and to cleanse us from all unrighteousness. Answer the call, open the door, invite the Holy One to come in and dine!

DAY 36 – PERFECT TIMING

1 Timothy 2:5-6 (ESV)

"For there is one God, and there is one mediator between God and men, the man Christ Jesus, who gave himself as a ransom for all, which is the testimony given at the proper time."

God's timing is always perfect, and nothing He has set in place can be moved or shifted unless He decides to do so Himself. The problem, which is really our problem, is that we often don't want to wait for God to act, and we take matters into our own hands. Even the cry of *"Hosanna"* is a cry for immediate delivery, a cry for God to *"save now."*

Messiah's sacrifice fulfilled a plan set in place before the foundation of the earth. Yet, its fulfillment didn't come until about four thousand years of human history had elapsed. We would have wanted Him to save us the moment Adam and Eve sinned, so as to avoid the years of trouble that proceeded. But Scripture says that Messiah's sacrifice was a testimony given at the proper time (1 Tim. 2:6).

Many of us are crying, *"Hosanna,"* today, especially as tensions between nations, people, and ethnicities threaten to explode into all-out war. We are crying, *"Hosanna,"* as tyrants of the world seek to get their hands on nuclear weapons and strong men of the nations talk of nuclear proliferation. Still, our salvation is for the proper time—a time already determined.

Yeshua said that Abraham saw His day and rejoiced (John 8:56). Abraham looked forward to a time when the Messiah would come but continued to live out his days in his time. So too shall we live out our days looking to the day when He returns. Until then, we must be vigilant to carry out the mission He has entrusted to us—to love the Lord, to love each other, to take His Gospel to the world, to teach others, and to baptize in the name of the Father, Son, and Holy Spirit (Matt. 28:19).

What is your role in this holy calling? You don't have to be a preacher, teacher, or a leader in the church in order to minister Yeshua. The Gospel is the good news, and we desperately need good news these days. Share your love with others and point them to Yeshua with your own life. Live the Gospel—the life ordained for us in the Scriptures—and Messiah will be glorified. Shine your light, and people will see the way they should go. Remember, darkness confuses our sense of direction. Only light can give us a clear sense of direction. Follow the Son; He will guide you to the promised land, and *let your light so shine before men, that they may see your good works and glorify your Father in Heaven"* (Matt. 5:16).

DAY 37 – SACRIFICE

2 Corinthians 5:21 (CJB)

"God made this sinless man be a sin offering on our behalf, so that in union with Him we might fully share in God's righteousness."

Animal sacrifice is still a reality in some modern-day cults, but not the major world religions—that is, until recently. The newly re-established Jewish Sanhedrin has re-instituted the sacrificial system—at least in part, as of this writing—which they have carried out at the foot of the temple mount in Jerusalem. This is in preparation for the expected third temple, without which they have long said the sacrifices are not allowed. When the temple stood, it was the only place one could offer up burnt offerings for the forgiveness of sins, offerings that had to be repeated time and again.

Yeshua is the sin offering for those who believe in Him, and His death on the execution stake was a sacrifice offered once for all time. You and I are made clean in His blood. Various Bible translations of Isaiah 52:15 say [Messiah] will sprinkle many nations. This is the picture of the High Priest sprinkling the blood of the sin offering on the sides of the altar.

We no longer have to travel to Jerusalem to offer up burnt offerings for the forgiveness of sins. Yeshua lifted that burden from us when He carried it to Golgotha. He carried our sins to the execution stake and said to us, *"I am the resurrection and the life. He who believes in Me, though he may die, he shall live"* (John 11:25). Fulfilling that promise to us is His resurrection from the dead. That is why the apostle Paul writes, *"Set your minds on things above, not on things on the earth. For you died, and your life is hidden with Messiah in God"* (Col. 3:2-4).

The price of our sins has been paid. We no longer need the blood of goats and bulls, but we must still bring a sacrifice of praise. We must bring our broken and contrite hearts to confess our sins and ask God to forgive our sins. We must believe on the Lord, Messiah Yeshua, for the remission of our sins. He is the Way, the Truth, and the Life by whom only do we have access to the Father.

DAY 38 – WHEN IS THERE SILENCE?

Malachi 4:1-6 (NKJV)

"'For behold, the day is coming, burning like an oven, and all the proud, yes, all who do wickedly will be stubble. And the day which is coming shall burn them up,' says the Lord of hosts, 'That will leave them neither root nor branch. But to you who fear My name the Sun of Righteousness shall arise with healing in His wings; and you shall go out and grow fat like stall-fed calves. You shall trample the wicked, for they shall be ashes under the soles of your feet on the day that I do this,' says the Lord of hosts. 'Remember the Law of Moses, My servant, which I commanded him in Horeb for all Israel, with the statutes and judgments. Behold, I will send you Elijah the prophet before the coming of the great and dreadful day of the Lord. And he will turn the hearts of the fathers to the children, and the hearts of the children to their fathers, lest I come and strike the earth with a curse.'"

The book of Malachi appears, in most translations, just before Matthew, making it the last book of the Old Testament. Many biblical scholars refer to this period between the testaments as the silent years, though one could argue that God is always speaking. During this time of great upheaval for the Jewish people, the Maccabean revolt took place, bringing us the Books of the Maccabees. While these have been deemed non-canonical, they provide a good historical overview of events that affected the people of God during that period—that which the angel told Daniel would be troublesome times.

There is another period of silence that we focus on during the Passover season. It is the short but agonizing stretch of days between the crucifixion and resurrection of Messiah Yeshua. Have you ever tried to imagine what was happening in the spiritual realm during that period? According to the apostle Peter:

> *Christ also died for sins once for all, the just for the unjust, so that He might bring us to God, having been put to death in the flesh, but made alive in the spirit; in which also He went and made proclamation to the spirits now in prison, who once were disobedient, when the patience of God kept waiting in the days of Noah, during the construction of the ark, in which a few, that is, eight persons, were brought safely through the water.*
>
> 1 Peter 3:18-20, NASB

Messiah Yeshua never stopped proclaiming the Gospel. What then should we do in times of reflection and contemplation? Should we seclude ourselves from the world to mourn the crucifixion of Messiah? No, we must be actively proclaiming His resurrection—His triumph over death and sin. We have been made alive in Messiah and must remain vigilant and active in the physical world as He is in the spiritual. The torch is ours to carry until that day comes, burning like an oven, to take away the proud and the wicked. Hold fast to Messiah and let His Holy Spirit carry you along. For even when the world does not see, He is still active, and although the world does not hear, He is still speaking.

DAY 39 – MESSIAH LIVES

Matthew 27:17-19 (NASB)

"As Jesus was about to go up to Jerusalem, He took the twelve disciples aside by themselves, and on the way He said to them, 'Behold, we are going up to Jerusalem; and the Son of Man will be delivered to the chief priests and scribes, and they will condemn Him to death, and will hand Him over to the Gentiles to mock and scourge and crucify Him, and on the third day He will be raised up.'"

D o you believe that Yeshua rose from the dead? This may seem an odd question, but there are many today who once believed Yeshua was just a mythical figure and who, as proof of His existence is uncovered, now say He was just a man who died and that is the end of it all. One may argue that it isn't so much that they don't believe as it is that they don't want to believe, because believing expects obedience.

The whole of Christianity and the Messianic community sits on the reality of Yeshua's birth, death, and resurrection; it is about what God did for us by stepping into His creation to redeem us from death. Belief in Messiah's death and resurrection is more than a mental exercise, for if we believe, we have a responsibility to obey. Partial obedience is disobedience, and those who choose which of Yeshua's commands to obey are living in disobedience to the Gospel.

Military rescue operation often includes a number of phases: (1) the rescue, (2) a rally point, and (3) an area designation for support teams to extract (pick up) the team and those rescued and bring them to a safe location.

Yeshua's death was a rescue operation. His resurrection and the present age is a rally point where we serve as missionaries and gate keepers until He returns to receive (extract) us to bring us to safety. Living conditions on this earth are not what we often wish they were, but this is our present reality, with the promise of a perfect tomorrow with our Lord. Yes, perfection is possible, but not by or through us. Only God is perfect, and only He can remake this world so that it will be perfect.

Today, live as one who is vital to the mission at hand, as one who is a vital member of a rescue team. Live to rescue those who are in spiritual bondage. Recognize and hold true to your role as one living among the saints at the rally point, waiting patiently for the day of our relocation and welcoming the newly rescued so that they may adjust to their new life in Messiah. Live in expectation of Yeshua's return and work diligently to prepare others for that wonderful event.

> *Do not let your heart be troubled; believe in*
> *God, believe also in Me. In My Father's house*
> *are many dwelling places; if it were not so, I*
> *would have told you; for I go to prepare a place*

for you. If I go and prepare a place for you, I will come again and receive you to Myself, that where I am, there you may be also.

John 14:1-3, NASB

DAY 40 – LIVING PROOF

Mark 16:1-6 (NKJV)

"Now when the Sabbath was past, Mary Magdalene, Mary the mother of James, and Salome bought spices, that they might come and anoint Him. Very early in the morning, on the first day of the week, they came to the tomb when the sun had risen. And they said among themselves, 'Who will roll away the stone from the door of the tomb for us?' But when they looked up, they saw that the stone had been rolled away—for it was very large. And entering the tomb, they saw a young man clothed in a long white robe sitting on the right side; and they were alarmed. But he said to them, 'Do not be alarmed. You seek Jesus of Nazareth, who was crucified. He is risen! He is not here. See the place where they laid Him.'"

There are many cultural practices we don't understand, but our lack of understanding doesn't nullify their truths. These three women were going to a tomb to anoint the body of a dead person after it had already been cleaned, wrapped in linen, and placed in a tomb behind a very large stone. They recognized their dilemma as they approached the tomb— *"Who will roll away the stone?"*

How often have you begun a journey only to realize you didn't account for apparent obstacles before heading out? It is often in times like this that God shows up to give us the help we need, even when we don't ask for it, and especially if what we are doing fulfills His purposes.

"He is risen!" declared the angel. *"See the place where they laid Him."* One can imagine that the women experienced varying emotions in this encounter, from one of relief when they saw the stone rolled away to astonishment and perplexity at the angel's proclamation. You and I don't have the advantage of looking into the tomb to see where they laid Yeshua—to see the linen cloth that encased His bruised body—but even the women probably could not grasp the full extent of what had just taken place.

"He is risen" is not just a fancy movie title or catch phrase; it is a reality that continues to baffle the "wise" among us. Yeshua said to Thomas, *"Blessed are they who have not seen and yet believe."* That is you, me, and everyone who did not see Yeshua before and in the days following His crucifixion.

Seeing or witnessing an event strengthens or solidifies our faith. This is evident in Thomas's response to Yeshua or the angel's invitation for the women to see the place where He was laid. Faith does not require proof, but we should not despise proof and the uncovering of evidence. In these last days, there will be much proof presented to the unbelieving culture. Let these proofs work to strengthen your faith, and do not rail against them, for though you have believed without seeing, others will be brought into the kingdom when they see.

Scripture tells us to *"taste and see that the Lord is good"* (Psalm 34:8). That Messiah is risen requires no proof for the faithful believer, but for those whose minds have been darkened and who struggle in their fight with the deceiver, proof is very necessary.

Today, be that proof that is so very necessary for the skeptic. Live a life so transformed by the resurrection of Messiah Yeshua that others will see it and marvel at its possibility. Be the evidence they need—those who seek proof to believe. We have been raised with Messiah, and His Spirit is within us. The angels of God point to the saints and say to those who seek Him: "See the place where He resides!"

The believer is the proof of His resurrection, for, as the apostle Paul says, *"If [Messiah] is not risen, then our preaching is empty and your faith is also empty"* (1 Cor. 15:14). The unbelieving world will continue to seek proof, even while proof is before their faces. Live a life that is only made possible by the work of Messiah Yeshua.

Live as one who is rescued from darkness and shine the light of Messiah which is in you. Live the proof, be the proof, and glorify God in your body so that at the day of judgement, they will not have an excuse. Every knee will bow, and every tongue will confess His lordship.

May Adonai bless you as you
continue your journey!

CPSIA information can be obtained
at www.ICGtesting.com
Printed in the USA
FSHW021400051119
63780FS

9 781545 681442